Step-by-Step, Practical Recipes Soups: Contents

Everyday Tasty Soups

These robust everyday soups can be served as a starter or a main meal. Some come with noodles, but most are delicious served with fresh crusty bread.

Hot & Spicy Soups

Soups are a big feature of cooking in the Far East, where they are often served as an all-in-one meal, with noodles or dumplings, meat or fish and plenty of spices!

FLAME TREE has been creating family-friendly, classic and beginner recipes for our bestselling cookbooks for over 12 years now. Our mission is to offer you a wide range of expert-tested dishes, while providing clear images of the final dish so that you can match it to your own results. We hope you enjoy this super selection of recipes – there are plenty more to try! Titles in this series include:

Cupcakes • Slow Cooker • Curries Chinese • Soups • Baking Breads Cakes • Simple Suppers • Pasta Chicken • Fish & Seafood • Chocolate

For more information please visit: *www.flametreepublishing.com*

Carrot & Ginger Soup

INGREDIENTS

Serves 4

4 slices of bread, crusts removed
1 tsp yeast extract
2 tsp olive oil
1 onion, peeled and chopped
1 garlic clove, peeled and crushed
½ tsp ground ginger
450 g/1 lb carrots, peeled
  and chopped
1 litre/1 ¾ pint vegetable stock
2.5 cm/1 inch piece of root ginger,
  peeled and finely grated
salt and freshly ground black pepper
1 tbsp lemon juice

To garnish:
chives
lemon zest

1 Preheat the oven to 180°C/350°F/Gas Mark 4. Roughly chop the bread. Dissolve the yeast extract in 2 tablespoons of warm water and mix with the bread.

2 Spread the bread cubes over a lightly oiled baking tray and bake for 20 minutes, turning halfway through. Remove from the oven and reserve.

3 Heat the oil in a large saucepan. Gently cook the onion and garlic for 3–4 minutes.

4 Stir in the ground ginger and cook for 1 minute to release the flavour.

5 Add the chopped carrots, then stir in the stock and the fresh ginger. Simmer gently for 15 minutes.

6 Remove from the heat and allow to cool a little. Blend until smooth, then season to taste with salt and pepper. Stir in the lemon juice. Garnish with the chives, bread and lemon zest; serve immediately.

TASTY TIP
For a special occasion, serve with a spoonful of lightly whipped cream or créme fraîche.

Mushroom & Sherry Soup

INGREDIENTS

Serves 4

4 slices day old white bread

zest of 1 lemon

1 tbsp lemon juice

salt and freshly ground black pepper

125 g/4 oz assorted wild mushrooms, lightly rinsed

125 g/4 oz baby button mushrooms, wiped

2 tsp olive oil

1 garlic clove, peeled and crushed

6 spring onions, trimmed and diagonally sliced

600 ml/1 pint chicken stock

4 tbsp dry sherry

1 tbsp freshly snipped chives, to garnish

HELPFUL HINT

To achieve very fine shreds of lemon zest, use a zester, obtainable from all kitchen shops. Or thinly peel the fruit with a vegetable peeler, then shred with a small sharp knife. When grating fruit, use a clean, dry pastry brush to remove the rind from the grater.

1 Preheat the oven to 180°C/350°F/Gas Mark 4. Remove the crusts from the bread and cut the bread into small cubes.

2 In a large bowl toss the cubes of bread with the lemon rind and juice, 2 tablespoons of water and plenty of freshly ground black pepper.

3 Spread the bread cubes on to a lightly oiled, large baking tray and bake for 20 minutes until golden and crisp.

4 If the wild mushrooms are small, leave some whole. Otherwise, thinly slice all the mushrooms and reserve.

5 Heat the oil in a saucepan. Add the garlic and spring onions and cook for 1–2 minutes.

6 Add the mushrooms and cook for 3–4 minutes until they start to soften. Add the chicken stock and stir to mix.

7 Bring to the boil, then reduce the heat to a gentle simmer. Cover and cook for 10 minutes.

8 Stir in the sherry, and season to taste with a little salt and pepper. Pour into warmed bowls, sprinkle over the chives, and serve immediately with the lemon croûtons.

2

4

6

Chinese Chicken Soup

INGREDIENTS

Serves 4

225 g/8 oz cooked chicken

1 tsp sesame oil

6 spring onions, trimmed and
   diagonally sliced

1 red chilli, deseeded and
   finely chopped

1 garlic clove, peeled and crushed

2.5 cm/1 inch piece root ginger,
   peeled and finely grated

1 litre/1³/₄ pints chicken stock

150 g/5 oz medium egg noodles

1 carrot, peeled and cut
   into matchsticks

125 g/4 oz beansprouts

2 tbsp soy sauce

1 tbsp fish sauce fresh coriander
   leaves, to garnish

TASTY TIP

To add nutritional value to this soup, substitute the egg noodles here with the wholewheat variety. Increase the vegetable content by adding 75 g/3 oz each of water chestnuts and bamboo shoots and 50 g/2 oz of sugar snap peas and baby corn in step 7.

1 Remove any skin from the chicken. Place on a chopping board and use two forks to tear the chicken into fine shreds.

2 Heat the oil in a large saucepan and fry the spring onions and chilli for 1 minute.

3 Add the garlic and ginger and cook for another minute.

4 Stir in the chicken stock and gradually bring the mixture to the boil.

5 Break up the noodles a little and add to the boiling stock with the carrot.

6 Stir to mix, then reduce the heat to a simmer and cook for 3–4 minutes.

7 Add the shredded chicken, beansprouts, soy sauce and fish sauce and stir.

8 Cook for a further 2–3 minutes until piping hot. Ladle the soup into bowls and sprinkle with the coriander leaves. Serve immediately.

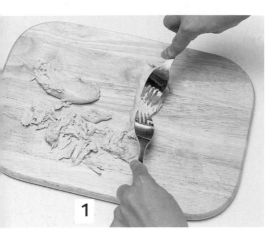

1

5

7

Italian Bean Soup

INGREDIENTS

Serves 4

2 tsp olive oil

1 leek, washed and chopped

1 garlic clove, peeled and crushed

2 tsp dried oregano

75 g/3 oz green beans, trimmed and
   cut into bite-size pieces

410 g can cannellini beans, drained
   and rinsed

75 g/3 oz small pasta shapes

1 litre/1 ³/₄ pint vegetable stock

8 cherry tomatoes

1 Heat the oil in a large saucepan. Add the leek, garlic and oregano and cook gently for 5 minutes, stirring occasionally.

2 Stir in the green beans and the cannellini beans. Sprinkle in the pasta and pour in the stock.

3 Bring the stock mixture to the boil, then reduce the heat to a simmer.

4 Cook for 12–15 minutes or until the vegetables are tender and the pasta is cooked to 'al dente'. Stir occasionally.

5 In a heavy-based frying pan, dry-fry the tomatoes over a high heat until they soften and the skins begin to blacken.

6 Gently crush the tomatoes in the pan with the back of a spoon and add to the soup.

7 Season to taste with salt and pepper. Stir in the shredded basil and serve immediately.

TASTY TIP

This soup tastes even better the day after it has been made. Make the soup the day before you intend serving it and add a little extra stock when reheating.

Tomato & Basil Soup

INGREDIENTS

Serves 4

1.1 kg/2½ lb ripe tomatoes,
 cut in half
2 garlic cloves
1 tsp olive oil
1 tbsp balsamic vinegar
1 tbsp dark brown sugar
1 tbsp tomato purée
300 ml/½ pint vegetable stock
6 tbsp natural yogurt
2 tbsp freshly chopped basil
salt and freshly ground black pepper
small basil leaves, to garnish

TASTY TIP

Use the sweetest type of tomatoes available as it will make a really big difference to the flavour of the soup. Many big supermarkets now stock speciality ranges, grown slowly and matured for longer on the vine to give them a more intense flavour. If these are unavailable, add a little extra sugar to bring out the flavour.

1 Preheat the oven to 200°C/400°F/Gas Mark 6. Evenly spread the tomatoes and unpeeled garlic in a single layer in a large roasting tin.

2 Mix the oil and vinegar together. Drizzle over the tomatoes and sprinkle with the dark brown sugar.

3 Roast the tomatoes in the preheated oven for 20 minutes until tender and lightly charred in places.

4 Remove from the oven and allow to cool slightly. When cool enough to handle, squeeze the softened flesh of the garlic from the papery skin. Place with the charred tomatoes in a nylon sieve over a saucepan.

5 Press the garlic and tomato through the sieve with the back of a wooden spoon.

6 When all the flesh has been sieved, add the tomato purée and vegetable stock to the pan. Heat gently, stirring occasionally.

7 In a small bowl beat the yogurt and basil together and season to taste with salt and pepper. Stir the basil yogurt into the soup. Garnish with basil leaves and serve immediately.

2

4

7

Curried Parsnip Soup

INGREDIENTS

Serves 4

1 tsp cumin seeds
2 tsp coriander seeds
1 tsp oil
1 onion, peeled and chopped
1 garlic clove, peeled and crushed
½ tsp turmeric
¼ tsp chilli powder
1 cinnamon stick
450 g/1 lb parsnips, peeled
  and chopped
1 litre/1 ¾ pint vegetable stock
salt and freshly ground black pepper
2–3 tbsp natural yogurt, to serve
fresh coriander leaves, to garnish

FOOD FACT

Parsnips vary in colour from pale yellow to a creamy white. They are at their best when they are the size of a large carrot. If larger, remove the central core which can be woody.

1   In a small frying pan, dry-fry the cumin and coriander seeds over a moderately high heat for 1–2 minutes. Shake the pan during cooking until the seeds are lightly toasted.

2   Reserve until cooled. Grind the toasted seeds in a pestle and mortar.

3   Heat the oil in a saucepan. Cook the onion until softened and starting to turn golden.

4   Add the garlic, turmeric, chilli powder and cinnamon stick to the pan. Continue to cook for a further minute.

5   Add the parsnips and stir well. Pour in the stock and bring to the boil. Cover and simmer for 15 minutes or until the parsnips are cooked.

6   Allow the soup to cool. Once cooled, remove the cinnamon stick and discard.

7   Blend the soup in a food processor until very smooth.

8   Transfer to a saucepan and reheat gently. Season to taste with salt and pepper. Garnish with fresh coriander and serve immediately with the yogurt.

1

5

6

Roasted Red Pepper, Tomato & Red Onion Soup

INGREDIENTS

Serves 4

2 tsp olive oil

2 large red peppers, deseeded
 and roughly chopped

1 red onion, peeled and
 roughly chopped

350 g/12 oz tomatoes, halved

1 small crusty French loaf

1 garlic clove, peeled

600 ml/1 pint vegetable stock

salt and freshly ground black pepper

1 tsp Worcestershire sauce

4 tbsp fromage frais

HELPFUL HINT

A quick, hassle-free way to remove the skin from peppers once they have been roasted or grilled is to place them in a polythene bag. Leave for 10 minutes or until cool enough to handle, then simply peel the skin away from the flesh.

1 Preheat the oven to 190°C/375°F/Gas Mark 5. Pour the oil into a large roasting tin and place the peppers and onion in the base, tossing to coat. Cook in the oven for 10 minutes. Add the tomatoes and cook for a further 20 minutes or until the peppers are soft.

2 Cut the bread into 1 cm/½ inch slices. Cut the garlic clove in half and rub the cut edge of the garlic over the bread.

3 Place all the bread slices on a large baking tray, and bake in the preheated oven for 10 minutes, turning halfway through, until golden and crisp.

4 Remove the vegetables from the oven and allow to cool slightly, then blend in a food processor until smooth. Strain the vegetable mixture through a large nylon sieve into a saucepan, to remove the seeds and skin. Add the stock, season to taste with salt and pepper and stir to mix. Heat the soup gently until piping hot.

5 In a small bowl beat together the Worcestershire sauce with the fromage frais.

6 Pour the soup into warmed bowls and swirl a spoonful of the fromage frais mixture into each bowl. Serve immediately with the garlic toasts.

1

4

5

Swede, Turnip, Parsnip & Potato Soup

INGREDIENTS

Serves 4

2 large onions, peeled

25 g/1 oz butter

2 medium carrots, peeled and
   roughly chopped

175 g/6 oz swede, peeled and
   roughly chopped

125 g/4 oz turnip, peeled and
   roughly chopped

125 g/4 oz parsnips, peeled and
   roughly chopped

175 g/6 oz potatoes, peeled

1 litre/1 3/4 pints vegetable stock

1/2 tsp freshly grated nutmeg

salt and freshly ground black pepper

4 tbsp vegetable oil, for frying

125 ml/4 fl oz double cream

warm crusty bread, to serve

1 Finely chop 1 onion. Melt the butter in a large saucepan and add the onion, carrots, swede, turnip, parsnip and potatoes. Cover and cook gently for about 10 minutes, without colouring. Stir occasionally during this time.

2 Add the stock and season to taste with the nutmeg, salt and pepper. Cover and bring to the boil, then reduce the heat and simmer gently for 15–20 minutes, or until the vegetables are tender. Remove from the heat and leave to cool for 30 minutes.

3 Heat the oil in a large heavy-based frying pan. Add the onions and cook over a medium heat, for about 2–3 minutes, stirring frequently, until golden brown. Remove the onions with a slotted spoon and drain well on absorbent kitchen paper. As they cool, they will turn crispy.

4 Pour the cooled soup into a food processor or blender and process to form a smooth purée. Return to the pan, adjust the seasoning, then stir in the cream. Gently reheat and top with the crispy onions. Serve immediately with chunks of bread.

HELPFUL HINT

For a slightly lower-fat version of this delicious soup, try adding milk (skimmed if preferred) rather than cream when reheating.

1

3

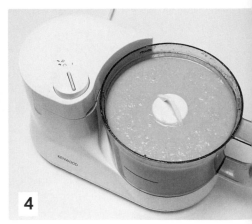
4

Potato & Fennel Soup

INGREDIENTS

Serves 4

25 g/1 oz butter
2 large onions, peeled and
   thinly sliced
2–3 garlic cloves, peeled and crushed
1 tsp salt
2 medium potatoes (about 450 g/1 lb
   in weight), peeled and diced
1 fennel bulb, trimmed and
   finely chopped
½ tsp caraway seeds
1 litre/1¾ pints vegetable stock
freshly ground black pepper
2 tbsp freshly chopped parsley
4 tbsp crème fraîche
roughly torn pieces of French stick,
   to serve

FOOD FACT

A fennel bulb is in fact the swollen stem of a fennel plant. One type of fennel, Florence fennel, comes from Italy and is used widely in Italian cooking. It has a distinct aniseed flavour, which mellows and sweetens when cooked. Look out for well-rounded bulbs with bright green fronds.

1 Melt the butter in a large heavy-based saucepan. Add the onions, with the garlic and half the salt, and cook over a medium heat, stirring occasionally, for 7–10 minutes, or until the onions are very soft and beginning to turn brown.

2 Add the potatoes, fennel bulb, caraway seeds and the remaining salt. Cook for about 5 minutes, then pour in the vegetable stock. Bring to the boil, partially cover and simmer for 15–20 minutes, or until the potatoes are tender. Stir in the chopped parsley and adjust the seasoning to taste.

3 For a smooth-textured soup, allow to cool slightly then pour into a food processor or blender and blend until smooth. Reheat the soup gently, then ladle into individual soup bowls. For a chunky soup, omit this blending stage and ladle straight from the saucepan into soup bowls.

4 Swirl a spoonful of crème fraîche into each bowl and serve immediately with roughly-torn pieces of French stick.

Potato, Leek & Rosemary Soup

INGREDIENTS

Serves 4

50 g/2 oz butter
450 g/1 lb leeks, trimmed and
   finely sliced
700 g/1½ lb potatoes, peeled and
   roughly chopped
900 ml/1½ pints vegetable stock
4 sprigs of fresh rosemary
450 ml/ ¾ pint full-cream milk
2 tbsp freshly chopped parsley
2 tbsp crème fraîche
salt and freshly ground black pepper
wholemeal rolls, to serve

TASTY TIP

This rosemary-scented version of Vichyssoise is equally delicious served cold. Allow the soup to cool before covering, then chill in the refrigerator for at least 2 hours. The soup will thicken as it chills, so you may need to thin it to the desired consistency with more milk or stock and season before serving. It is important to use fresh rosemary rather than dried for this recipe.

1 Melt the butter in a large saucepan, add the leeks and cook gently for 5 minutes, stirring frequently. Remove 1 tablespoon of the cooked leeks and reserve for garnishing.

2 Add the potatoes, vegetable stock, rosemary sprigs and milk. Bring to the boil, then reduce the heat, cover and simmer gently for 20–25 minutes, or until the vegetables are tender.

3 Cool for 10 minutes. Discard the rosemary, then pour into a food processor or blender and blend well to form a smooth-textured soup.

4 Return the soup to the saucepan and stir in the chopped parsley and crème fraîche. Season to taste with salt and pepper. If the soup is too thick, stir in a little more milk or water. Reheat gently without boiling, then ladle into warm soup bowls. Garnish the soup with the reserved leeks and serve immediately with wholemeal rolls.

1

2

4

Cream of Spinach Soup

INGREDIENTS

Serves 6–8

1 large onion, peeled and chopped

5 large plump garlic cloves, peeled and chopped

2 medium potatoes, peeled and chopped

750 ml/1¼ pints cold water

1 tsp salt

450 g/1 lb spinach, washed and large stems removed

50 g/2 oz butter

3 tbsp flour

750 ml/1¼ pints milk

½ tsp freshly grated nutmeg

freshly ground black pepper

6–8 tbsp crème fraîche or soured cream

warm foccacia bread, to serve

HELPFUL HINT

When choosing spinach, always look for fresh, crisp, dark green leaves. Use within 1–2 days of buying and store in a cool place. To prepare, wash in several changes of water to remove any dirt or grit and shake off as much excess water as possible.

1 Place the onion, garlic and potatoes in a large saucepan and cover with the cold water. Add half the salt and bring to the boil. Cover and simmer for 15–20 minutes, or until the potatoes are tender. Remove from the heat and add the spinach. Cover and set aside for 10 minutes.

2 Slowly melt the butter in another saucepan, add the flour and cook over a low heat for about 2 minutes. Remove the saucepan from the heat and add the milk, a little at a time, stirring continuously. Return to the heat and cook, stirring continuously, for 5–8 minutes, or until the sauce is smooth and slightly thickened. Add the freshly grated nutmeg to taste.

3 Blend the cooled potato and spinach mixture in a food processor or blender to a smooth purée, then return to the saucepan and gradually stir in the white sauce. Season to taste with salt and pepper and gently reheat, taking care not to allow the soup to boil. Ladle into soup bowls and top with spoonfuls of crème fraîche or soured cream. Serve immediately with warm foccacia bread.

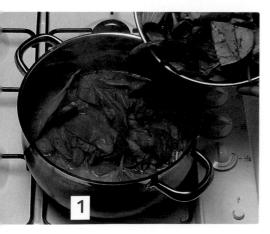

Rice Tomato Soup

INGREDIENTS

Serves 4

150 g/5 oz easy-cook basmati rice
400 g can chopped tomatoes
2 garlic cloves, peeled and crushed
grated rind of ½ lime
2 tbsp extra virgin olive oil
1 tsp sugar
salt and freshly ground pepper
300 ml/½ pint vegetable stock
   or water

For the croûtons:
2 tbsp prepared pesto sauce
2 tbsp olive oil
6 thin slices ciabatta bread, cut into
   1 cm/½ inch cubes

TASTY TIP

Pesto is a vivid green sauce, made from basil leaves, garlic, pine nuts, Parmesan cheese and olive oil. Shop-bought pesto is fine for this quick soup, but try making your own during the summer when basil is plentiful.

1 Preheat the oven to 220°C/425°F/Gas Mark 7. Rinse and drain the basmati rice. Place the canned tomatoes with their juice in a large heavy-based saucepan with the garlic, lime rind, oil and sugar. Season to taste with salt and pepper. Bring to the boil, then reduce the heat, cover and simmer for 10 minutes.

2 Add the boiling vegetable stock or water and the rice, then cook, uncovered, for a further 15–20 minutes, or until the rice is tender. If the soup is too thick, add a little more water. Reserve and keep warm, if the croûtons are not ready.

3 Meanwhile, to make the croûtons, mix the pesto and olive oil in a large bowl. Add the bread cubes and toss until they are coated completely with the mixture. Spread on a baking sheet and bake in the preheated oven for 10–15 minutes, until golden and crisp, turning them over halfway through cooking. Serve the soup immediately sprinkled with the warm croûtons.

Coconut Chicken Soup

INGREDIENTS

Serves 4

2 lemon grass stalks
3 tbsp vegetable oil
3 medium onions, peeled and
  finely sliced
3 garlic cloves, peeled and crushed
2 tbsp fresh root ginger, finely grated
2–3 kaffir lime leaves
1½ tsp turmeric
1 red pepper, deseeded and diced
400 ml can coconut milk
1.1 litres/2 pints vegetable or
  chicken stock
275 g/9 oz easy-cook long-grain rice
275 g/10 oz cooked chicken meat
285 g can sweetcorn, drained
3 tbsp freshly chopped coriander
1 tbsp Thai fish sauce
freshly chopped pickled chillies,
  to serve

1 Discard the outer leaves of the lemon grass stalks, then place on a chopping board and, using a mallet or rolling pin, pound gently to bruise; reserve.

2 Heat the vegetable oil in a large saucepan and cook the onions over a medium heat for about 10–15 minutes until soft and beginning to change colour.

3 Lower the heat, stir in the garlic, ginger, lime leaves and turmeric and cook for 1 minute. Add the red pepper, coconut milk, stock, lemon grass and rice. Bring to the boil, cover and simmer gently over a low heat for about 10 minutes.

4 Cut the chicken into bite-sized pieces, then stir into the soup with the sweetcorn and the freshly chopped coriander. Add a few dashes of the Thai fish sauce to taste, then reheat gently, stirring frequently. Serve immediately with a few chopped pickled chillies to sprinkle on top.

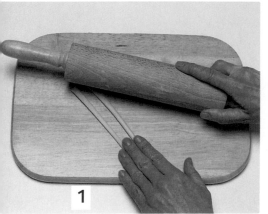

1

3

4

Bacon & Split Pea Soup

INGREDIENTS

Serves 4

50 g/2 oz dried split peas
25 g/1 oz butter
1 garlic clove, peeled and
   finely chopped
1 medium onion, peeled and
   thinly sliced
175 g/6 oz long-grain rice
2 tbsp tomato purée
1.1 litres/2 pints vegetable or
   chicken stock
175 g/6 oz carrots, peeled and
   finely diced
125 g/4 oz streaky bacon,
   finely chopped
salt and freshly ground black pepper
2 tbsp freshly chopped parsley
4 tbsp single cream
warm crusty garlic bread, to serve

1 Cover the dried split peas with plenty of cold water, cover loosely and leave to soak for a minimum of 12 hours, preferably overnight.

2 Melt the butter in a heavy-based saucepan, add the garlic and onion and cook for 2–3 minutes, without colouring. Add the rice, drained split peas and tomato purée and cook for 2–3 minutes, stirring constantly to prevent sticking. Add the stock, bring to the boil, then reduce the heat and simmer for 20–25 minutes, or until the rice and peas are tender. Remove from the heat and leave to cool.

3 Blend about three-quarters of the soup in a food processor or blender to form a smooth purée. Pour the purée into the remaining soup in the saucepan. Add the carrots to the saucepan and cook for a further 10–12 minutes, or until the carrots are tender.

4 Meanwhile, place the bacon in a non-stick frying pan and cook over a gentle heat until the bacon is crisp. Remove and drain on absorbent kitchen paper.

5 Season the soup with salt and pepper to taste, then stir in the parsley and cream. Reheat for 2–3 minutes, then ladle into soup bowls. Sprinkle with the bacon and serve immediately with warm garlic bread.

2

3

3

Pumpkin & Smoked Haddock Soup

INGREDIENTS

Serves 4–6

2 tbsp olive oil

1 medium onion, peeled and chopped

2 garlic cloves, peeled and chopped

3 celery stalks, trimmed and chopped

700 g/1¼ lb pumpkin, peeled,
   deseeded and cut into chunks

450 g/1 lb potatoes, peeled and cut
   into chunks

750 ml/1¼ pints chicken
   stock, heated

125 ml/4 fl oz dry sherry

200 g/7 oz smoked haddock fillet

150 ml/¼ pint milk

freshly ground black pepper

2 tbsp freshly chopped parsley

1 Heat the oil in a large heavy-based saucepan and gently cook the onion, garlic, and celery for about 10 minutes. This will release the sweetness but not colour the vegetables. Add the pumpkin and potatoes to the saucepan and stir to coat the vegetables with the oil.

2 Gradually pour in the stock and bring to the boil. Cover, then reduce the heat and simmer for 25 minutes, stirring occasionally. Stir in the dry sherry, then remove the saucepan from the heat and leave to cool for 5–10 minutes.

3 Blend the mixture in a food processor or blender to form a chunky purée and return to the saucepan.

4 Meanwhile, place the fish in a shallow frying pan. Pour in the milk with 3 tablespoons of water and bring to almost boiling point. Reduce the heat, cover and simmer for 6 minutes, or until the fish is cooked and flakes easily. Remove from the heat and, using a slotted spoon, remove the fish from the liquid, reserving both liquid and fish.

5 Discard the skin and any bones from the fish and flake into pieces. Stir the fish liquid into the soup, together with the flaked fish. Season with freshly ground black pepper, stir in the parsley and serve immediately.

TASTY TIP

For this soup, try to find undyed smoked haddock rather than the brightly coloured yellow type. The texture and flavour are much better.

Clear Chicken & Mushroom Soup

INGREDIENTS

Serves 4

2 large chicken legs, about 450 g/1 lb
  total weight
1 tbsp groundnut oil
1 tsp sesame oil
1 onion, peeled and very thinly sliced
2.5 cm/1 inch piece root ginger,
  peeled and very finely chopped
1.1 litres/2 pints clear chicken stock
1 lemon grass stalk, bruised
50 g/2 oz long-grain rice
75 g/3 oz button mushrooms, wiped
  and finely sliced
4 spring onions, trimmed, cut into
  5 cm/2 inch pieces and shredded
1 tbsp dark soy sauce
4 tbsp dry sherry
salt and freshly ground black pepper

1   Skin the chicken legs and remove any fat. Cut each in half to make two thigh and two drumstick portions and reserve. Heat the groundnut and sesame oils in a large saucepan. Add the sliced onion and cook gently for 10 minutes, or until soft but not beginning to colour.

2   Add the chopped ginger to the saucepan and cook for about 30 seconds, stirring all the time to prevent it sticking, then pour in the stock. Add the chicken pieces and the lemon grass, cover and simmer gently for 15 minutes. Stir in the rice and cook for a further 15 minutes or until the chicken is cooked.

3   Remove the chicken from the saucepan and leave until cool enough to handle. Finely shred the flesh, then return to the saucepan with the mushrooms, spring onions, soy sauce and sherry. Simmer for 5 minutes, or until the rice and mushrooms are tender. Remove the lemon grass.

4   Season the soup to taste with salt and pepper. Ladle into warmed serving bowls, making sure each has an equal amount of shredded chicken and vegetables and serve immediately.

FOOD FACT

Tahini is a rich, thick paste made from sesame seeds. It is available from many delicatessens and supermarkets as well as Oriental food stores. It is most often used in making houmous.

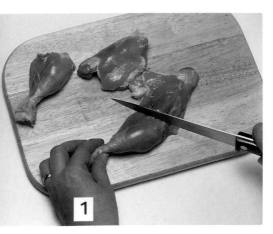

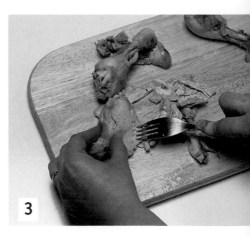

Wonton Noodle Soup

INGREDIENTS

Serves 4

4 shiitake mushrooms, wiped

125 g/4 oz raw prawns, peeled and
  finely chopped

125 g/4 oz pork mince

4 water chestnuts, finely chopped

4 spring onions, trimmed and
  finely sliced

1 medium egg white

salt and freshly ground black pepper

1½ tsp cornflour

1 packet fresh wonton wrappers

1.1 litres/2 pints chicken stock

2 cm/¾ inch piece root ginger,
  peeled and sliced

75 g/3 oz thin egg noodles

125 g/4 oz pak choi, shredded

FOOD FACT

Wonton wrappers are thin, almost see-through sheets of dough made from eggs and flour, about 10 cm/4 inches square. You can buy them fresh or frozen from larger supermarkets and Asian stores.

1 Place the mushrooms in a bowl, cover with warm water and leave to soak for 1 hour. Drain, remove and discard the stalks and finely chop the mushrooms. Return to the bowl with the prawns, pork, water chestnuts, 2 of the spring onions and egg white. Season to taste with salt and pepper. Mix well.

2 Mix the cornflour with 1 tablespoon of cold water to make a paste. Place a wonton wrapper on a board and brush the edges with the paste. Drop a little less than 1 teaspoon of the pork mixture in the centre then fold in half to make a triangle, pressing the edges together. Bring the two outer corners together, fixing together with a little more paste. Continue until all the pork mixture is used up; you should have 16–20 wontons.

3 Pour the stock into a large, wide saucepan, add the ginger slices and bring to the boil. Add the wontons and simmer for about 5 minutes. Add the noodles and cook for 1 minute. Stir in the pak choi and cook for a further 2 minutes, or until the noodles and pak choi are tender and the wontons have floated to the surface and are cooked through.

4 Ladle the soup into warmed bowls, discarding the ginger. Sprinkle with the remaining sliced spring onion and serve immediately.

Wonton Soup

INGREDIENTS

Serves 6

For the chicken stock:

900 g/2 lb chicken or chicken pieces
  with back, feet and wings
1–2 onions, peeled and quartered
2 carrots, peeled and chopped
2 celery stalks, trimmed and chopped
1 leek, trimmed and chopped
2 garlic cloves, unpeeled and
  lightly crushed
1 tbsp black peppercorns
2 bay leaves
small bunch parsley, stems only
2–3 slices fresh root ginger,
  peeled (optional)
3.4 litres/6 pints cold water

For the soup:

18 wontons
2–3 Chinese leaves, or a handful of
  spinach, shredded
1 small carrot, peeled and cut
  into matchsticks
2–4 spring onions, trimmed and
  diagonally sliced
soy sauce, to taste
handful of flat leaf parsley, to garnish

1 Chop the duck into 6–8 pieces and put into a large stock pot or saucepan of water with the remaining stock ingredients. Place over a high heat and bring to the boil, skimming off any scum which rises to the surface. Reduce the heat and simmer for 2–3 hours, skimming occasionally.

2 Strain the stock through a fine sieve into a large bowl. Leave to cool, then chill in the refrigerator for 5–6 hours, or overnight. When cold, skim off the fat and remove any remaining small pieces of fat by dragging a piece of absorbent kitchen paper lightly across the surface.

3 Bring a medium saucepan of water to the boil. Add the wontons and return to the boil. Simmer for 2–3 minutes, or until the wontons are cooked, stirring frequently. Rinse under cold running water, drain and reserve.

4 Pour 300 ml/½ pint stock per person into a large wok. Bring to the boil over a high heat, skimming any foam that rises to the surface and simmer for 5–7 minutes to reduce slightly. Add the wontons, Chinese leaves or spinach, carrots and spring onions. Season with a few drops of soy sauce and simmer for 2–3 minutes. Garnish with a few parsley leaves and serve immediately.

Prawn & Chilli Soup

INGREDIENTS

Serves 4

2 spring onions, trimmed

225 g/8 oz whole raw tiger prawns

750 ml/1¼ pint fish stock

finely grated rind and juice of 1 lime

1 tbsp fish sauce

1 red chilli, deseeded and chopped

1 tbsp soy sauce

1 lemon grass stalk

2 tbsp rice vinegar

4 tbsp freshly chopped coriander

1 To make spring onion curls, finely shred the spring onions lengthways. Place in a bowl of iced cold water and reserve.

2 Remove the heads and shells from the prawns leaving the tails intact.

3 Split the prawns almost in two to form a butterfly shape and individually remove the black thread that runs down the back of each one.

4 In a large pan, heat the stock with the lime rind and juice, fish sauce, chilli and soy sauce.

5 Bruise the lemon grass by crushing it along its length with a rolling pin, then add to the stock mixture.

6 When the stock mixture is boiling, add the prawns and cook until they are pink.

7 Remove the lemon grass and add the rice vinegar and coriander.

8 Ladle into bowls and garnish with the spring onion curls. Serve immediately.

TASTY TIP

For a more substantial dish, cook 50–75 g/2–3 oz Thai fragrant rice for 12–15 minutes, or until just cooked. Drain, then place a little in the soup bowl and ladle the prepared soup on top.

1

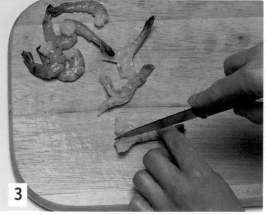

3

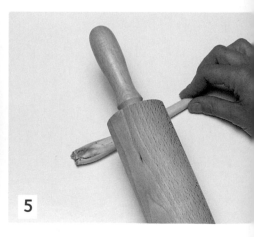

5

Hot-&-Sour Mushroom Soup

INGREDIENTS

Serves 4

4 tbsp sunflower oil

3 garlic cloves, peeled and
   finely chopped

3 shallots, peeled and finely chopped

2 large red chillies, deseeded and
   finely chopped

1 tbsp soft brown sugar

large pinch of salt

1 litre/1¾ pints vegetable stock

250 g/9 oz Thai fragrant rice

5 kaffir lime leaves, torn

2 tbsp soy sauce

grated rind and juice of 1 lemon

250 g/9 oz oyster mushrooms, wiped
   and cut into pieces

2 tbsp freshly chopped coriander

To garnish:

2 green chillies, deseeded and
   finely chopped

3 spring onions, trimmed and
   finely chopped

1 Heat the oil in a frying pan, add the garlic and shallots and cook until golden brown and starting to crisp. Remove from the pan and reserve. Add the chillies to the pan and cook until they start to change colour.

2 Place the garlic, shallots and chillies in a food processor or blender and blend to a smooth purée with 150 ml/¼ pint water. Pour the purée back into the pan, add the sugar with a large pinch of salt, then cook gently, stirring, until dark in colour. Take care not to burn the mixture.

3 Pour the stock into a large saucepan, add the garlic purée, rice, lime leaves, soy sauce and the lemon rind and juice. Bring to the boil, then reduce the heat, cover and simmer gently for about 10 minutes.

4 Add the mushrooms and simmer for a further 10 minutes, or until the mushrooms and rice are tender. Remove the lime leaves, stir in the chopped coriander and ladle into bowls. Place the chopped green chillies and spring onions in small bowls and serve separately to sprinkle on top of the soup.

1

2

4

Thai Hot-&-Sour Prawn Soup

INGREDIENTS

Serves 6

700 g/1½ lb large raw prawns

2 tbsp vegetable oil

3–4 stalks lemon grass, outer leaves
discarded and coarsely chopped

2.5 cm/1 inch piece fresh root ginger,
peeled and finely chopped

2–3 garlic cloves, peeled and crushed

small bunch fresh coriander, leaves
stripped and reserved, stems
finely chopped

½ tsp freshly ground black pepper

1.8 litres/3¼ pints water

1–2 small red chillies, deseeded and
thinly sliced

1–2 small green chillies, deseeded
and thinly sliced

6 kaffir lime leaves, thinly shredded

4 spring onions, trimmed and
diagonally sliced

1–2 tbsp Thai fish sauce

1–2 tbsp freshly squeezed lime juice

1. Remove the heads from the prawns by twisting away from the body and reserve. Peel the prawns, leaving the tails on and reserve the shells with the heads. Using a sharp knife, remove the black vein from the back of the prawns. Rinse and dry the prawns and reserve. Rinse and dry the heads and shells.

2. Heat a wok, add the oil and, when hot, add the prawn heads and shells, the lemon grass, ginger, garlic, coriander stems and black pepper and stir-fry for 2–3 minutes, or until the prawn heads and shells turn pink and all the ingredients are coloured.

3. Carefully add the water to the wok and return to the boil, skimming off any scum which rises to the surface. Simmer over a medium heat for 10 minutes or until slightly reduced. Strain through a fine sieve and return the clear prawn stock to the wok.

4. Bring the stock back to the boil and add the reserved prawns, chillies, lime leaves and spring onions and simmer for 3 minutes, or until the prawns turn pink. Season with the fish sauce and lime juice. Spoon into heated soup bowls, dividing the prawns evenly and float a few coriander leaves over the surface.

FOOD FACT

Thai fish sauce, which is made from fermented anchovies, has a very strong sour, salty, fishy flavour.

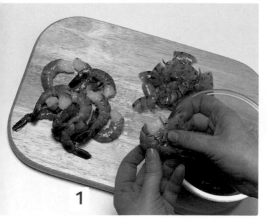

1

2

4

Creamy Caribbean Chicken & Coconut Soup

INGREDIENTS

Serves 4

6–8 spring onions
2 garlic cloves
1 red chilli
175 g/6 oz cooked chicken,
  shredded or diced
2 tbsp vegetable oil
1 tsp ground turmeric
300 ml/½ pint coconut milk
900 ml/1½ pints chicken stock
50 g/2 oz small soup pasta or
  spaghetti, broken into small pieces
½ lemon, sliced
salt and freshly ground black pepper
1–2 tbsp freshly chopped coriander
sprigs of fresh coriander, to garnish

HELPFUL HINT

Be careful handling chillies. Either wear rubber gloves or scrub your hands thoroughly, using plenty of soap and water. Avoid touching eyes or any other sensitive areas.

1 Trim the spring onions and thinly slice; peel the garlic and finely chop. Cut off the top of the chilli, slit down the side and remove seeds and membrane, then finely chop and reserve.

2 Remove and discard any skin or bones from the cooked chicken, shred using two forks and reserve.

3 Heat a large wok, add the oil and when hot add the spring onions, garlic and chilli and stir-fry for 2 minutes, or until the onion has softened. Stir in the turmeric and cook for 1 minute.

4 Blend the coconut milk with the chicken stock until smooth, then pour into the wok. Add the pasta or spaghetti with the lemon slices and bring to the boil.

5 Simmer, half-covered, for 10–12 minutes, or until the pasta is tender; stir occasionally.

6 Remove the lemon slices from the wok and add the chicken. Season to taste with salt and pepper and simmer for 2–3 minutes, or until the chicken is heated through thoroughly.

7 Stir in the chopped coriander and ladle into heated bowls. Garnish with sprigs of fresh coriander and serve immediately.

2

3

6

Hot-&-Sour Soup

INGREDIENTS

Serves 4-6

25 g/1 oz dried Chinese
(shiitake) mushrooms

2 tbsp groundnut oil

1 carrot, peeled and cut
into julienne strips

125 g/4 oz chestnut mushrooms,
wiped and thinly sliced

2 garlic cloves, peeled and
finely chopped

½ tsp dried crushed chillies

1.1 litres/2 pints chicken stock

75 g/3 oz cooked boneless chicken
or pork, shredded

125 g/4 oz fresh bean curd,
thinly sliced, optional

2–3 spring onions, trimmed and
finely sliced diagonally

1–2 tsp sugar

3 tbsp cider vinegar

2 tbsp soy sauce

salt and freshly ground black pepper

1 tbsp cornflour

1 large egg

2 tsp sesame oil

2 tbsp freshly chopped coriander

1 Place the dried Chinese (shiitake) mushrooms in a small bowl and pour over enough almost-boiling water to cover. Leave for 20 minutes to soften, then gently lift out and squeeze out the liquid. (Lifting out the mushrooms leaves any grit behind.) Discard the stems and thinly slice the caps and reserve.

2 Heat a large wok, add the oil and, when hot, add the carrot strips and stir-fry for 2–3 minutes, or until beginning to soften. Add the chestnut mushrooms and stir-fry for 2–3 minutes or until golden, then stir in the garlic and chillies.

3 Add the chicken stock to the vegetables and bring to the boil, skimming off any foam that rises to the surface. Add the shredded chicken or pork, bean curd, if using, spring onions, sugar, vinegar, soy sauce and reserved Chinese mushrooms and simmer for 5 minutes, stirring occasionally. Season to taste with salt and pepper.

4 Blend the cornflour with 1 tablespoon of cold water to form a smooth paste and whisk into the soup. Return to the boil and simmer over a medium heat until thickened.

5 Beat the egg with the sesame oil and slowly add to the soup in a slow, steady stream, stirring constantly. Stir in the chopped coriander and serve the soup immediately.

Step-by-Step, Practical Recipes Soups: Tips & Hints

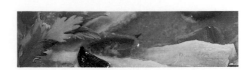

Tasty Tip

Though you can use a shop bought stocks for making soups, it is important that it is a good quality one. For the best results, you can make your own stock – you will really notice the difference! A fresh chicken stock can be made by boiling the left-over carcass of a roast chicken with seasoning, some herbs, such as a bayleaf and some thyme, and a carrot. At the end, sieve and use straight away, or refrigerate. You can also use an ice-tray to freeze the stock in small portions for use when needed.

Food Fact

There is evidence to suggest that soup, in some form, has been around since 6000 BC. More recently, it has become a mainstay of most cuisines, providing nutritious, cheap meals. It is incredibly versatile and comes in a huge range of styles, from all over the world; from French Vichyssoise (see p20) to Chinese Wonton Soup (see p36).

Helpful Hint

Invest in a hand-held blender or food processor. They can be bought quite cheaply these days from the major supermarkets or online. Depending on the type of soup you are making, soups can be quite chunky, with the ingredients still whole; for example, many Far-Eastern soups, such as ones from Thailand or China, are served like a small stew, with meat, vegetables and noodles all still intact. Some of the more everyday, European-style soups are also served in this way. However, there are many soups that comes as a delicious blended, smooth purée-like soup, such as Curried Parsnip Soup (see p12) or Carrot and Ginger Soup (see p2).

Tasty Tip

Using freshly bought ingredients is best with most types of cooking, but even more so for soups, which generally have less ingredients than some other dishes and so rely more on the quality of the main ingredients for flavour. Having said that, soups can also be a way of economising and using up vegetables that you might be about to throw away. As a rule, the fresher the ingredients the better the flavour, but it is up to you how you prioritise flavour over economy.

Tasty Tip

A good way to add bulk to your soups, and so transform them into a meal in their own right, is to add pulses or beans – this is great if you are trying to keep your costs down. Dried beans and pulses, such as split peas (see p28), will need to be soaked and perhaps cooked beforehand, though some brands of dried lentils are designed to be used directly. Dried pulses and beans are also cheapest. Slightly more expensive are tinned beans and pulses such as butter beans, flageolet beans, cannellini beans (see p8) and lentils, which are not as tasty as dried varieties cooked at home, but are more convenient to use. You should only add these shortly before the end of the cooking time, as they are already cooked and disintegrate if 'reheated' for too long.

Food Fact

Croûtons are small cubes of bread, that are either baked in the oven or fried in a small amount of olive oil in a pan. You can give them a bit more flavour by adding seasonings such as herbs, grated parmesan or pesto. They are also very tasty with just a little sea salt. Croûtons can be used to add flavour and bulk to some of the soups listed in this book, for example, Carrot and Ginger Soup (see p2). They are also a really great way to use up slightly stale bread that would otherwise be wasted!

Food Fact

French Onion soup is one of the most classic soups of all time! It consists of onions in a beef broth topped with big croûtons and gruyère cheese. Onion soups have been popular since Roman times and have been eaten throughout history by poorer people, since onions are easily grown and cheap and plentiful. The classic modern version came into being in France in the 18th century.

Helpful Hint

Fish (see p30) make a really nutritious addition to soups. They can also be expensive so, to save money, try using a mixture of expensive and cheap fish – the cheaper fish can be used to add flavour.

First published in 2012 by
FLAME TREE PUBLISHING LTD
Crabtree Hall, Crabtree Lane, Fulham,
London, SW6 6TY, United Kingdom
www.flametreepublishing.com

The CIP record for this book is available from the British Library • Printed in China

NOTE: Recipes using uncooked eggs should be avoided by infants, the elderly, pregnant women and anyone suffering from an illness.

18 17 16 15 14 13 12   10 9 8 7 6 5 4 3 2 1

ISBN: 978-0-85775-609-1

ACKNOWLEDGEMENTS: Authors: Catherine Atkinson, Juliet Barker, Gina Steer, Vicki Smallwood, Carol Tennant, Mari Mererid Williams, Elizabeth Wolf-Cohen and Simone Wright. Photography: Colin Bowling, Paul Forrester and Stephen Brayne. Home Economists and Stylists: Jacqueline Bellefontaine, Mandy Phipps, Vicki Smallwood and Penny Stephens. All props supplied by Barbara Stewart at Surfaces. Publisher and Creative Director: Nick Wells. Editorial: Catherine Taylor, Sarah Goulding, Marcus Hardie, Gina Steer and Karen Fitzpatrick. Design and Production: Chris Herbert, Mike Spender, Colin Rudderham and Helen Wall.